NATIONAL GEOGRAPHIC

Ladders

BIG STORM

HURRICANE

THEY THOUGHT THEY WERE GOING TO DIE.

Floodwaters quickly swallowed up the family car near Bay St. Louis, Mississippi. The Taylor family huddled together on the only safe place—the roof of their SUV. There, they waited to be rescued.

KATRINA

by Christopher Siegel

A volunteer rescue crew finally arrived. Finally, the Taylors
were safe from Hurricane Katrina. What causes "big storms" like
hurricanes to form? What is it like to live through such a storm?

KATRINA'S PATH

Hurricanes are powerful storms that form over warm ocean water. On August 23, 2005, the conditions were just right over the Bahamas. Warm water from the Atlantic Ocean began to **evaporate.** Moist air rose quickly into the sky. It cooled and **condensed,** or changed into tiny droplets of water. These droplets formed storm clouds. The clouds came together. Thunderstorms formed. Then many thunderstorms joined together into one giant storm. The giant storm began to spin like a huge carousel in the sky. It was big enough to be given a name—Katrina. Look at Katrina's path as it developed into a hurricane. It moved toward Florida, and then into the Gulf of Mexico.

MONDAY, AUGUST 29

At 6:10 a.m., Katrina slams into one of the largest coastal cities—New Orleans, Louisiana.

New Orleans

Gulf of Mexico

SATURDAY, AUGUST 27

Hurricane Katrina heads toward the coasts of Mississippi and Louisiana.

This satellite image shows Hurricane Katrina as seen from space.

THURSDAY, AUGUST 25

The storm is now a hurricane. It is named Hurricane Katrina. A hurricane warning is issued for the Florida coast. Katrina passes near Miami, Florida. By midnight, over one million homes lose power and 11 lives are lost.

FRIDAY, AUGUST 26

Hurricane Katrina moves into the Gulf of Mexico. The storm becomes bigger and stronger.

WEDNESDAY, AUGUST 24

Swirling storm clouds grow stronger over the Bahamas. At this time, the storm is only a tropical storm.

Miami

Bahamas

Cuba

Water quickly filled the streets. People who could not evacuate sought shelter in places above the raging flood.

KATRINA HITS

The sky darkened as Katrina made landfall. Buckets of rain came down. Howling winds blew. The storm lifted mounds of ocean water and moved it toward the coast. The huge storm measured about 400 kilometers (248 miles) from end to end. Katrina's winds reached speeds of 278 kilometers (173 miles) per hour. Katrina swamped areas close to the coast with waters over 5 meters (16 feet) high. That's almost twice the height of the stop signs in New Orleans! Katrina was one of the worst storms to ever hit the Gulf Coast.

NEW ORLEANS UNDERWATER

One of the largest cities hit by Katrina was New Orleans, Louisiana.

Although evacuation warnings were issued, many residents did not have time to leave. As Katrina barreled through the city, people tried to find shelter. But Katrina was a much more powerful storm than was **forecasted.**

Worse still, most of New Orleans is below sea level. This means that the land is lower than the surrounding waterways. Manmade walls and barriers called **levees** usually protect the land. But the flooding from Katrina was too much for the levees. Many of them broke. The floodwater raged into the city. In a matter of seconds, homes and possessions were swept away. Tens of thousands of people became homeless. Entire neighborhoods were destroyed. Sadly, many people lost their lives.

Hurricane Katrina caused several levees to break. Water rushed in. Floods covered much of New Orleans.

REBUILDING A COMMUNITY

New Orleans's Lower Ninth Ward had the most damage. This once stable neighborhood was quickly swamped. The levees protecting the neighborhood broke and water was everywhere. However, survivors are determined to make a comeback! One resident said, "I have to come home. I have to rebuild . . . because it's my home."

Soon brightly colored homes started to appear. But these are no ordinary homes. The new homes of the Lower Ninth are built to withstand future hurricanes. They are built high off the ground. They are supported by concrete pillars, so floodwater can pass under the homes.

Rebuilding the Lower Ninth and other parts of New Orleans and the Gulf Coast will take a long time. But residents of the Gulf Coast plan to reclaim their neighborhoods. The "big storm" of 2005 will never be forgotten, but because new buildings should withstand future hurricanes, the area is making a strong comeback.

"WHEN THE WATER CAME IN EVERYTHING WAS WIPED AWAY, INCLUDING LIVES. I NEVER WOULD HAVE THOUGHT THAT WE WOULD HAVE BEEN BACK HERE, **BUT WE ARE.**"

Check In In what ways did Hurricane Katrina impact the Gulf Coast?

PROTECTING New Orleans

by Richard Easby

"Can New Orleans be protected from future hurricanes?"

Many people were asking this question during the cleanup of Hurricane Katrina. You see, New Orleans is built on land that is mostly below sea level. The water in surrounding lakes and rivers is over 2.5 meters (8 feet) above some city streets. Better **levees** had to be built to protect the city. The United States Army Corps of Engineers made $14.5 billion worth of improvements to the levees. Would the new levees hold up to another big storm like Katrina?

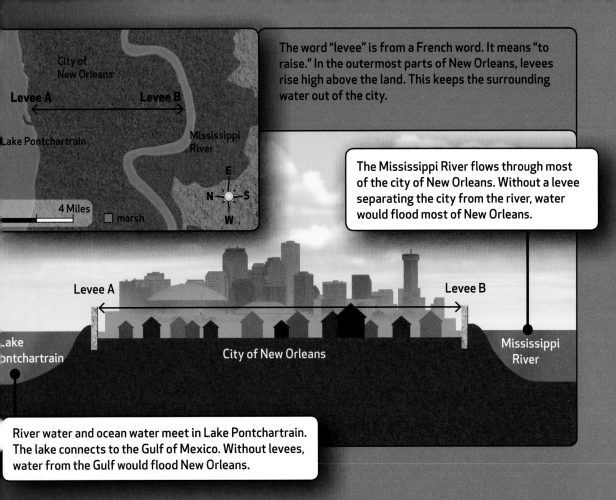

City of New Orleans

Levee A ←——————→ Levee B

Lake Pontchartrain

Mississippi River

E
N ⊕ S
W

4 Miles

☐ marsh

The word "levee" is from a French word. It means "to raise." In the outermost parts of New Orleans, levees rise high above the land. This keeps the surrounding water out of the city.

The Mississippi River flows through most of the city of New Orleans. Without a levee separating the city from the river, water would flood most of New Orleans.

Levee A ←——————→ Levee B

Lake Pontchartrain

City of New Orleans

Mississippi River

River water and ocean water meet in Lake Pontchartrain. The lake connects to the Gulf of Mexico. Without levees, water from the Gulf would flood New Orleans.

Rebuilding the new levees took many steps. First, crews had to find the best location. Next, they built a strong foundation. It would support the walls of the new levees.

They then used concrete and steel to build levee walls. Some of the new levee walls are about 7 meters (23 feet) high. The new levees are designed to hold up to future hurricanes.

Isaac's IMPACT

Almost seven years after Hurricane Katrina struck, Hurricane Isaac slammed the Gulf Coast. It was late August, 2012. Weather **forecasts** predicted that Isaac would hit land in New Orleans. This storm would test the new levee system. So did the new levees hold?

Well, it turned out that Isaac was not as powerful as Katrina. New Orleans was safe this time!

However, other areas along the Gulf Coast became flooded from Isaac. So, there is still more to be done before the whole area around New Orleans is protected from big storms.

The levee wall should prevent water from reaching land during a flood.

The new levees are made of concrete and steel. They are strong. A hurricane cannot easily knock them down.

Walls in the new levee system are almost 7 meters (23 feet).

The land next to the concrete wall is mounded with soil and rocks.

This is an aerial view of the Lower Ninth Ward. The new levee system includes concrete walls. New homes can be seen in the neighborhood.

Check In What steps have been taken to protect New Orleans since Hurricane Katrina?

Into the Eye of a Hurricane

by Stacey Klaman

< Major Deeann Lufkin and
Lieutenant Colonel Greg Lufkin.

A unit of the United States Air Force tracks hurricanes. The unit is made up of pilots and **meteorologists,** or scientists who track weather. They are called the Hurricane Hunters. The Hurricane Hunters fly into a hurricane. They use technology to collect information about a storm. They help the National Hurricane Center (NHC) better **forecast** storms. Read this interview with Lieutenant Colonel (LTC) Greg Lufkin, Squadron Commander of the Hurricane Hunters, and Major Deeann Lufkin, one of the unit's meteorologists.

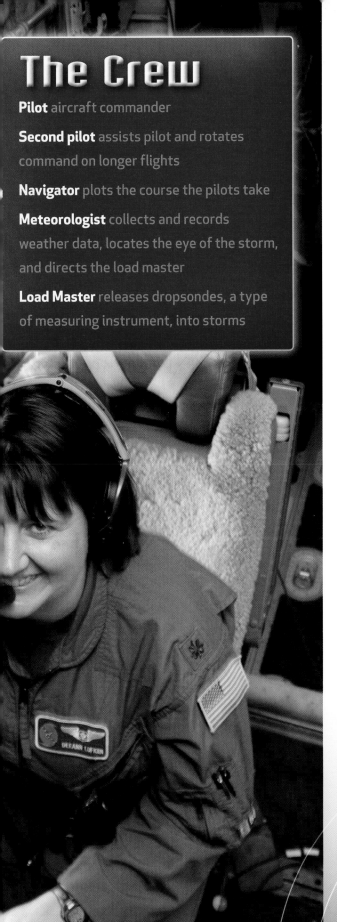

The Crew

Pilot aircraft commander

Second pilot assists pilot and rotates command on longer flights

Navigator plots the course the pilots take

Meteorologist collects and records weather data, locates the eye of the storm, and directs the load master

Load Master releases dropsondes, a type of measuring instrument, into storms

National Geographic: Why did you become a Hurricane Hunter?

Major Lufkin: When I was nine, I saw my first tornado. That's when I fell in love with weather. In college I studied weather and knew I wanted to be a Hurricane Hunter. I reached my goal when I joined the Air Force Reserves.

NG: What is it like to fly into a hurricane?

Major Lufkin: It is pretty bumpy. It feels like you are driving on a dirt road. But once inside the eye, the storm's walls fall silent for miles. Actually, it's really beautiful.

Major Deeann Lufkin sits at the controls aboard the Hurricane Hunter plane.

National Geographic:
How can you see inside
a hurricane wall?

LTC Lufkin: You can't. It's
raining so hard. The clouds
are so thick that you can't
see more than half an inch in
front of the window.

NG: How do you safely get
from one end of the hurricane
to the other?

LTC Lufkin: As the
navigator, it's my job to
direct the pilots. Using data
from color weather radar,
I tell the pilots the best
course to steer the
plane through
the storm.

LTC Greg Lufkin and Major Deeann Lufkin sit at their stations aboard the Hurricane Hunter plane.

The Hurricane Hunter plane has a wingspan of 39.7 meters (132 feet, 7 inches). Weather measuring devices are mounted on the plane's wings.

NG: How does the work of the Hurricane Hunters improve the accuracy of storm forecasts?

Major Lufkin: From a weather satellite in space, a hurricane looks like a big blob of clouds. The Hurricane Hunters fly much lower than a satellite. We fly at an altitude of 3,048 meters (10,000 feet). Our data is more accurate than a satellite's data. The information we send to the NHC improves overall storm and hurricane forecasts.

National Geographic:
What is your job on board
a mission?

Major Lufkin: The
plane's computers measure
temperature, air pressure,
wind speed, and humidity.
They do this twice every
second. I review the data and
send it to the NHC every ten
minutes. It's also my job to
find the storm's center. When
I do, I tell the load master
where to drop a dropsonde
into the storm.

NG: How does a dropsonde
improve forecasts?

Major Lufkin: A 'sonde'
nose-dives down through the
storm's eye or eyewall. It takes
more accurate measurements
than the plane. The sonde
sends data back to us four
times a second. I review the
data and then instant message
it to the NHC.

A dropsonde is loaded into the release chamber.
Then it is dropped into a storm. >

Hurricane Technology

Hurricane Hunters use high-tech instruments to get information. One instrument is the dropsonde. It is a tube that holds a radio and other sensing tools. A parachute opens up when a dropsonde is launched. It slows down the sonde as it falls. Hurricane Hunters drop about 12 sondes during a storm.

∨ Dropsondes are used to take weather measurements of the inside of hurricanes.

∧ There are different weather-measuring devices inside a dropsonde.

< A parachute allows the dropsonde to fall to Earth slowly.

National Geographic: How does the NHC use data from the Hurricane Hunters?

Major Lufkin: Their meteorologists put the data into computer models. The models help forecast a storm's direction. This helps the NHC issue more accurate warnings about the storm to the public.

NG: What do you like most about being a Hurricane Hunter?

Major Lufkin: Knowing that I'm helping people and potentially saving lives. That's pretty big. You can't do that with just any job.

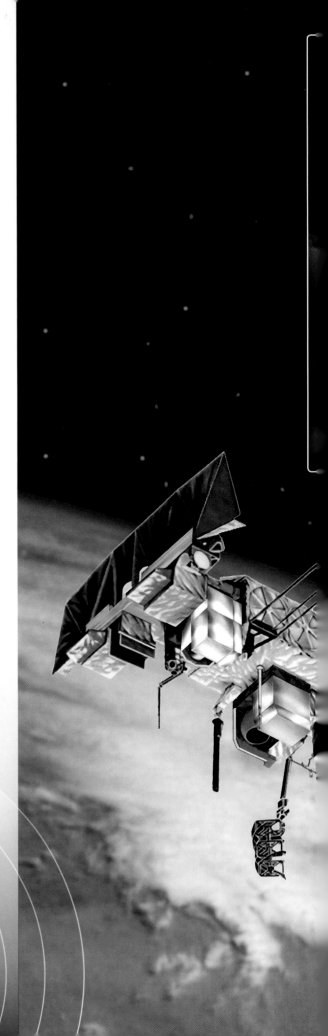

Improving Hurricane Forecasts

Scientists are working to improve hurricane forecasts. One project is called the Cyclone Global Navigation Satellite System (CYGNSS). It is a group of satellites that will be sent into space. The project is being developed by NASA and research teams at the University of Michigan. The satellites will give information about how hurricanes form. This will help meteorologists to forecast storms. More accurate forecasts will help keep people safe.

Thanks to advances in technology and the brave men and women of the Hurricane Hunters, we will be better prepared for hurricanes.

∧ Rockets are used to launch weather satellites into space.

∧ This artist illustration shows the CYGNSS as it would be seen in space.

Check In What other questions would you ask the Lu⁻

Discuss

1. Describe the sequence of events of Hurricane Katrina.

2. Discuss with a partner the steps that were taken after Katrina to prevent future problems of flooding in New Orleans.

3. How does the interview with the Hurricane Hunters relate to the other selections?

4. What information do meteorologists, such as the Hurricane Hunters, provide to better understand weather?

5. What other information do you want to learn about hurricanes? Where could you find answers to your questions?